CUP OF PRAYERS

PRAYERS THAT BREAK YOKES

EVELYN M. TOLBERT

Contents

About Cup Of Prayers,   ix
Prayers That Break Yokes
Introduction   xi

1. Prayer Against The Spirit Of Delay   1
   Praise And Worship
2. Prayer Against The Spirit Of Manipulation   6
   Praise And Worship
3. Prayer Against Generational Curses   9
   Praise And Worship
4. Prayer Against Diseases   13
   Praise And Worship
5. Prayer Against The Spirit Of Rejection   16
   Praise And Worship
6. Prayers Against Evil Arrows   19
   Praise And Worship

7. Prayers Against Monitoring Spirit — 23
Praise And Worship

8. Prayer Against Deceiving Spirit — 26
Praise And Worship

9. Prayer Against Evil Plot Or Plan Of The Enemy — 30
Praise And Worship

10. Prayers Against Destiny Robbers — 34
Praise And Worship

About the Author — 39

Copyright © 2020 by Evelyn M. Tolbert

All rights reserved.

Published by Firebrand Publishing Atlanta, GA USA

No part of this book may be reproduced in any form or by any electronic or mechanical means, including information storage and retrieval systems, without written permission from the author, except for the use of brief quotations in a book review and certain other noncommercial uses permitted by copyright law.

For permission requests, write to the publisher, addressed "Attention: Permissions coordinator," at the email address: support@firebrandpublishing.com

Limit of Liability/Disclaimer of Warranty: While the publisher and author have used their best efforts in preparing this book, they make no representations or warranties with respect to the accuracy or completeness of the contents of this book and specifically disclaim any implied warranties of merchantability or fitness for a particular purpose. No warranty may be created or extended by sales representatives or written sales materials. The advice and strategies contained herein may not be suitable for your situation. You should consult with a professional where appropriate. Neither the publisher nor the author shall be liable for damages arising here from.

Firebrand Publishing publishes in a variety of print and electronic formats and by print-on-demand. For more information about Firebrand Publishing products, visit https://firebrandpublishing.com

All Scriptures are taken from the NKJV except where stated.

ISBN: 978-1-941907-21-4 (paperback)

ISBN: 978-1-941907-22-1 (ebook)

Printed in the United States of America

To The Holy Spirit, the director and instructor of my life.

To all those who serve faithfully and selflessly in the kingdom.

To my late husband Willie B. Tolbert who was my rock, the one who always encouraged and supported me to be the best I can be in life.

To all my children and grandchildren who give me joy each and every day.

About Cup Of Prayers, Prayers That Break Yokes

If you find yourself burdened by demonic forces or evil yokes in your life ranging from generational curses, the spirit of rejection, or evil attacks, pray these prayers and receive your breakthrough from God.

Cup of Prayers, Prayers that break yokes is a daily devotional that helps break the evil yokes affecting your life through prayer.

Use this collection of prayers to break evil yokes, destroy demonic forces affecting your life, writs and more. Don't despair, there is power in prayer.

God answers prayers. All you need to do is call upon Him, and He will answer you.

Introduction

We are commanded to pray. There is power in prayer. Prayer changes things. Prayer makes you get closer to God.

> *Then He spoke a parable to them, that men always ought to pray and not lose heart.*
>
> Luke 18:1

Feed your spirit with the word of God and prayer daily, and see your spiritual life grow.

And you will seek Me and

> *find Me, when you search for Me, with all your heart.*
>
> Jeremiah 29:12

Then you will call upon Me and go and pray to Me, and I will listen to you.

> *I called on the LORD in distress, The LORD answered me and set me in a broad place.*
>
> Psalm 118:5

God answers prayers. All you need to do is call upon Him, and He will answer you.

Have praise and worship before each prayer session. Give Him praise, glorify Him for who He is, and all that He has done for you.

1

Prayer Against The Spirit Of Delay
PRAISE AND WORSHIP

There are different types of delays. Divine delay, self-delay, and satanic delay.

Divine delay is when God wants us to wait. There is nothing you can do about that, because He allows it. He does that for your own good.

The self-delay is the one you are responsible for delaying events in your life.

The satanic delay is the one caused by the enemy. The enemy can cause several kinds of delay in your life.

There is also delay in marriage, in child bearing, in academic achievement, in financial growth, spiritual growth, and many other delays in life. There is the spirit that brings roadblocks, obstacles, and hinders your progress. slowing down your vision in life.

In the book of Daniel, Daniel prayed and God answered. It took twenty one days for him to receive the answer to the prayer, because the Prince of Persia held the angel who was bringing the answer to him.

> *Then he said to me, "Do not fear, Daniel, for from the first day that you set your heart to understand, and to humble yourself before your God, your words were heard; and I have come because of your words. But the prince of the kingdom of Persia withstood me twenty-one days; and behold, Michael, one of the chief*

princes, came to help me, for I had been left alone there with the kings of Persia.

Daniel 10:12-13

1. Lion of the tribe of Judah, destroy every spirit of setback in my destiny, be destroyed by fire in the name of Jesus.

2. O Lord, every spirit of delay holding me back from achieving my goals, be consumed by Holy Ghost fire in the name of Jesus.

3. O Lord, the spirit of delay against my getting married be cancelled by fire, in the name of Jesus.

4. O Lord, every road block, and obstacle hindering me from achieving my financial goals, be removed from my destiny by Holy Ghost fire, in the name of Jesus.

5. O Lord, whatever power stopping me from having children be exterminated by fire, in the name of Jesus.

6. Fire of God, level every mountain that has been an obstacle to my lifting in life, in the name of Jesus.

7. O Lord, any power slowing down my vision in life be destroyed by Holy Ghost fire, in the name of Jesus.

8. O Lord, every of Your spoken words regarding my life and destiny shall come to manifestation, there shall be no more delay in my life, in the name of Jesus.

> *For I am the LORD, I speak, and the word I speak will come to pass, it will no more be postponed; for in your days, O rebellious house, I will say the word and perform it, says the LORD God.*
>
> Ezekiel 12:25

9. O Lord, I declare and decree every power that is not allowing me to be fruitful in life be consumed by fire, in the name of Jesus.

10. I declare and decree I shall not be delayed to get to my destination, in the name of Jesus.

2

Prayer Against The Spirit Of Manipulation
PRAISE AND WORSHIP

Manipulation is the act of controlling someone to your own advantage. The act of changing the behavior of others through deceptive or underhanded tactics. The following prayers are against spiritual manipulation, where you are being manipulated in the spirit realm without your knowledge.

> *For Satan himself*
> *transformed himself into*
> *an angel of light.*
> *And no wonder! For Satan*

himself transforms himself into an angel of light.

2 Corinthians 11:14

"Beware of false prophets, who come to you in sheep's clothing, but inwardly they are ravenous wolves."

Matthew 7:15

1. O Lord, every spirit of manipulation dwelling in my destiny be consumed by fire, in Jesus name.

2. O God my Father, whoever is manipulating my life, and hindering me from achieving my goals, be destroyed by Holy Ghost fire, in the name of Jesus.

3. Fire of God, burn to ashes every satanic power that is controlling my life in the spirit

realm, in the name of Jesus.

4. I cancel every spirit of manipulation in my life, and in the life of my family, in Jesus name.

5. O Lord, disconnect me from every evil manipulator in my destiny, in the name of Jesus.

6. Every demonic power manipulating the life of my children not to succeed, be roasted by fire in the name of Jesus.

7. O Lord, every manipulating power assigned to change my destiny, let that power die by Holy Ghost fire, in the name of Jesus.

8. O Lord, evil powers of my father's house manipulating my destiny be destroyed by Holy Ghost fire, in the name of Jesus.

9. Every power assigned to turn my glory to shame die by fire, in the name of Jesus.

10. O Lord, my glory shall not be manipulated, my glory shall rise in the name of Jesus.

3

Prayer Against Generational Curses
PRAISE AND WORSHIP

There are generational curses that sometimes follow you around in life, that are passed from your generations, affecting your destiny. There are curses you've inherited because of the offenses of your forefathers.

Reuben was cursed by his father Jacob because he slept with his father's concubine. Reuben was long gone, but the curse followed his descendants, who had no knowledge of his deed.

It took Moses to reverse the curse against Reuben's generations.

> "Let Reuben live, and not die, Nor let his men be few."
>
> Deuteronomy 33:6

The good news is that you can be free from generational curses when you pray the targeted prayers.

> *Christ has redeemed us from the curse of the law, having become a curse for us (for it is written, "Cursed is everyone who hangs on a tree").*
>
> Galatians 3:13

> *Stand fast therefore in the liberty by which Christ has made us free, and do not be entangled again with a yoke of bondage.*
>
> Galatians 5:1

1. O Lord, break every generational curse of poverty, and barrenness in my life and my children's lives, in the name of Jesus.

2. O Lord, I disconnect myself, and my descendants from all evil covenants from my father's house, and my mother's house, in the name of Jesus.

3. O Lord, I decree and declare that the generational curse of childlessness and diseases be broken, in the name of Jesus.

4. O Lord, I renounce any form of idolatry, traditions, and evil covenants from my father and mother's house, affecting my life in the name of Jesus.

5. By the power of the blood, I break every curse affecting my marriage, finances and progress, in the name of Jesus.

6. O Lord, every spoken curse against my destiny be broken by fire of God, in the name of Jesus.

7. I break every curse of slavery in my family bloodline, in the name of Jesus.

8. O Lord, I decree and declare that from today, I exercise my faith in the blood of Jesus, and release myself and descendants from every generational curse affecting our lives, in the name of Jesus.

9. O Lord, I will not suffer for the sins of my father and mother's house, in the name of Jesus.

10. I decree and declare freedom from every evil agreement or covenants made by my ancestors, in the name of Jesus.

Prayer Against Diseases
PRAISE AND WORSHIP

Isaiah 53:5

But He was wounded for our transgressions, He was bruised for our iniquities; The chastisement for our peace was upon Him, and by His stripes we are healed

> *For I will restore health to you and heal you of your wounds, says the LORD*
>
> Jeremiah 30:17

God is a healer, He is the Great Physician. He is Jehovah Rapha and can heal you of all your infirmities. Some need physical healing and some spiritual healing. Whatever your infirmity is, the Great Physician will give you total healing.

1. O Lord, whatever is in me that you have not deposited in me be flushed out by the blood of Jesus, in the name of Jesus.

2. O Lord, let the blood of Jesus heal me from any form of illness, be it physical, mental or spiritual in the name of Jesus.

3. O Lord, I bind the spirit of incurable diseases in my life and my family's lives in the name of Jesus.

4. O Lord, no form of plague or pestilence that walks in the darkness shall come near our dwelling place, in the name of Jesus

5. Lion of the tribe of Judah, I cover myself and my family with the blood of Jesus and no evil shall come near us, in the name of Jesus.

6. O Lord, any strange elements in my body that you did not create with me, let it be flushed out by the blood of Jesus.

7. O Lord, let the power in the blood heal any diseases in my body, in the name of Jesus.

8. O Lord, uproot every plant that you did not plant in me, by the blood of Jesus.

9. I decree and declare total healing and restoration in my body, in the name of Jesus.

10. O Lord, whatever contamination is in my body, by the blood of Jesus flush it out and heal me, in the name of Jesus.

> *Bless the LORD, O my soul,*
> *and forget not His*
> *benefits.*
>
> Psalm 103:2-3

Who forgives all your iniquities, who heals all your diseases.

Prayer Against The Spirit Of Rejection
PRAISE AND WORSHIP

We all want to belong and be accepted, either by family members, friends, or a group. Rejection is hurtful, and can make you feel that you are of no value. Let me tell you, that you are of value to God. You can be rejected because of your belief in God. You can also be rejected by family members. Whatever form of rejection you are facing, I pray that the Lord will remove that spirit of rejection from your life.

*When my father and my
mother forsake me . Then*

> *the Lord will take care of me.*
>
> Psalm 27:10

> *Blessed are you when men hate you, and when they exclude you, and revile you, and cast out your name as evil, for the Son of Man's sake.*
>
> Luke 6:22

1. O Lord, every spirit of rejection following me, be removed by Holy Ghost fire, in the name of Jesus.

2. O Lord, every spirit of rejection inherited from my father or mother's house be cast out from my destiny, in the name of Jesus.

3. O Lord, every mark of rejection following me around be removed, by the blood of Jesus.

4. O Lord, I renounce every form of rejection in my life and destiny, in Jesus name.

5. O Lord, I cancel every spirit of rejection operating in my life, in the name of Jesus.

6. O Lord, uproot and destroy every spirit of rejection that dwells in me, in the name of Jesus.

7. I decree and declare that everywhere I have been rejected, I shall be accepted back, in the name of Jesus.

8. O Lord, I break every spirit of rejection in my life, in the name of Jesus.

9. O Lord, I command the spirit of rejection to leave my life, in Jesus name.

10. Every power making me to be rejected wherever I go, be terminated by fire, in the name of Jesus.

6

Prayers Against Evil Arrows
PRAISE AND WORSHIP

The enemy can fire evil arrows at you in the spiritual realm without you knowing, and they can be deadly, depending on the purpose of the arrow. It can be the arrow of death, affliction, poverty etc. You may not even know that an evil arrow was fired at you, but you will feel the effect of it, in the natural.

> *For we do not wrestle against flesh and blood, but against principalities, against powers, against*

rulers of darkness of this age, against spiritual hosts of wickedness in the heavenly places.

Ephesians 6:12

You shall hide them in the secret place of Your presence, from the plots of man; You shall keep them secretly in a pavilion, from the strife of tongues.

Psalm 31:20

1. O Lord, return back to sender every evil arrow fired at me, in the name of Jesus.

2. O Lord, every arrow of confusion, and poverty fired at me, be returned back to sender by Holy Ghost fire, in the name of Jesus.

3. O Lord, let the terror of God rain against every enemy planning on firing evil arrows against my life, in the name of Jesus.

4. Every arrow of affliction fired into my destiny be returned to the sender by Holy Ghost fire, in the name of Jesus.

5. O Lord, I cancel every arrow of disappointment, and barrenness fired into my womb, in the name of Jesus.

6. Let the arrows of problems, sorrows, and trouble fired at my destiny, backfire in the name of Jesus.

7. O Lord, hide me in Your secret place, from the plots of evil men, in the name of Jesus.

8. Lion of the tribe of Judah, any arrow of death fired at me or my family, be fired back to sender by Holy Ghost fire, in the name of Jesus.

9. O Lord of preservation, shield me from the arrows of the enemy and preserve my life, in the name of Jesus.

10. Any evil arrows fired at any of my children, backfire in the name of Jesus.

7

Prayers Against Monitoring Spirit
PRAISE AND WORSHIP

In this, the twenty-first century, there are cameras everywhere. You are being watched, everywhere you go. We have cameras in our cell phones, the government has cameras all over the place. We have become accustomed to that, in our everyday life. You never knowwho is watching you. But I am talking about enemies that monitor your life in the spirit, without you knowing that you're being watched. Those who can see all of your progress in life and plot against it in the spiritual realm.

Now it happened, as we

> *went to prayer, that a certain slave girl possessed with a spirit of divination met us, who brought her masters much profit by fortune-telling.*
>
> Acts 16:16-17

This girl followed Paul and us, and cried out, saying, "These men are the servants of the Most High God, who proclaim to us the way of salvation."

1. O Lord, every satanic agent assigned to watch and report all of my movement or progress be exposed and paralyzed by Holy Ghost fire, in the name of Jesus.

2. O Lord, every evil meeting summoned against me be scattered by Holy Ghost fire, in the name of Jesus.

3. O Lord, every tongue uttering curses or evil pronouncement against my life be cut

off by fire, in the name of Jesus.

4. O Lord, any monitoring spirit setting traps for me shall fall into that same trap, in the name of Jesus.

5. O Lord, every demonic eye assigned to monitor my destiny be given blindness by fire, in the name of Jesus.

6. I bind every monitoring power tracking my destiny and progress in life, in the name of Jesus.

7. Every spiritual mirror being used against me, be broken by Holy Ghost fire, in the name of Jesus.

8. O Lord, break and destroy any spiritual gadgets being used to watch my life, in the name of Jesus.

9. I break every monitoring instrument fashioned against me and my family, in the name of Jesus.

10. Every power watching me in the spiritual realm, wishing me failure, catch fire in the name of Jesus.

8

Prayer Against Deceiving Spirit
PRAISE AND WORSHIP

In the natural, there are people that are deceivers. You can be deceived by friends or family members. In this book I am speaking about a deceitful spirit. You can be close to someone for many years and do not know their true identity. You can also be deceived, by fellow believers. The Bible says we should test all spirits.

> *For many believers have gone*
> *out into the world who*
> *do not confess Jesus*
> *Christ as coming in the*

> flesh. This is a deceiver and an antichrist.
>
> 2 John 7

> Beloved, do not believe every spirit, but test the spirits, whether they are of God; because many false prophets have gone out into the world.
>
> 1 John 4:1

1. O Lord, disconnect me from every deceiver in my life, in the name of Jesus.

2. O Lord, protect me from every deceiving spirit in my destiny, in the name of Jesus.

3. O Lord, I reject every deceiving spirit that wants to dwell in my mind, heart, and soul, in the name of Jesus.

4. O Lord, expose and destroy every deceiver around me, in the name of Jesus.

5. O Lord, do not allow me to be fooled or deceived by false doctrines, in the name of Jesus.

6. O Lord, remove from my life every deceiver, in the name of Jesus.

7. O Lord, I will not be deceived by lying or deceitful tongues, in the name of Jesus.

8. I disconnect myself and my family from every deceiving man or woman, in the name of Jesus.

9. Every deceiving spirit in my life that is affecting my success, I terminate your assignment in the name of Jesus.

10. I command every deceiver in my family's life to be exposed, and their agenda be destroyed by Holy Ghost fire, in the name of Jesus.

Let no one deceive you by any means; for that day will not come unless the falling away comes first, and the man of sin is revealed, the son of perdition.

2 Thessalonians 2:3

Prayer Against Evil Plot Or Plan Of The Enemy
PRAISE AND WORSHIP

thus says the Lord God: "It shall not stand, Nor shall it come to pass."

Isaiah 7:7

1. O Lord, every evil plot or plan against me and my family shall not come to pass, in the name of Jesus.

2. O Lord, let my enemies arise against themselves and attack each other, in the name of Jesus.

> *So they rose early in the morning and went out into the Wilderness of Tekoa; and as they went out, Jehoshaphat stood and said, "Hear me, O Judah and you inhabitants of Jerusalem: Believe in the Lord your God, and you shall be established; believe His prophets, and you shall prosper."*
>
> 2 Chronicles 20:20

3. O Lord, send your axe of fire into the camp of the enemies gathering against me, in the name of Jesus.

4. Lion of the tribe of Judah, the plan and plot of the enemy against my destiny shall not stand and shall not come to manifestation, in the name of Jesus.

5. O Lord, every evil conspiracy against me or my family, be exposed and cancelled in the name of Jesus.

6. O Lord, let the wicked fall by their own wickedness, in the name of Jesus.

> *The righteousness of the blameless will direct his way aright,*
> *But the wicked will fall by his own wickedness.*
>
> Proverbs 11:5

7. O Lord, let the evil expectation of the enemy against my life perish by fire, in the name of Jesus.

> *When a wicked man dies, his expectation will perish,*
> *And the hope of the unjust perishes.*
>
> Proverbs 11:7

8. O Lord, hide me in Your secret place from the plot of evil men, in the name of Jesus.

9. O Lord arise and destroy by fire every evil parasite dwelling in my home, in the name of Jesus.

10. O Lord, disconnect me from every evil agenda, and connect me with a divine agenda, in the name of Jesus.

Prayers Against Destiny Robbers
PRAISE AND WORSHIP

We all have a destiny. Some are destined to be great, regardless of what happens to them in life. There are others that are supposed to be great, but enemies either alter their destiny, attack their destiny, or steal their destiny. There are destiny attackers, destiny robbers, destiny destroyers, but there are also destiny helpers.

> *"Before I formed you in the womb I knew you; Before you were born I sanctified you; I ordained*

you a prophet to the nations."

Jeremiah 1:5

And we know that all things work together for good to those who love God, for those who are called according to His purpose.

Romans 8:28

1. O Lord, on this earth I shall not labor in vain, in the name of Jesus.

2. Every agent of darkness assigned to destroy my destiny, let them catch fire in the name of Jesus.

3. O Lord, every stronghold of darkness against my destiny, be destroyed by Holy Ghost fire, in the name of Jesus.

4. Power of God, consume by fire every power assigned to alter my destiny, in the name of Jesus.

5. Every destiny attacker assigned to attack my destiny, be paralyzed by the power of God, in the name of Jesus.

6. O Lord, expose and destroy all destiny robbers in my life, in the name of Jesus.

7. Every evil agenda programmed to alter my destiny, be cancelled by fire, in the name of Jesus.

8. Every power contending with my destiny, be scattered by fire, in the name of Jesus.

9. I declare and decree total freedom from every satanic agent holding me hostage, in the name of Jesus.

10. Every satanic chain that has chained me down, be broken by Holy Ghost fire, in Jesus name.

*Now to Him who is able to
do exceedingly
abundantly above all*

> *that we ask or think, according to the power that works in us,*
>
> Ephesians 3:20

To Him be glory in the church by Christ Jesus to all generations forever and ever. Amen.

May the Lord answer all your prayers. I pray that every yoke be broken, and burden be lifted, in the mighty name of Jesus Christ.

About the Author

EVELYN M. TOLBERT is the Pastor and founder of Divine Promise Ministry located in Georgia. She is a dynamic leader, a teacher of the word and a devoted mother and grandmother. She was married to the late Willie Tolbert.

www.ingramcontent.com/pod-product-compliance
Lightning Source LLC
Chambersburg PA
CBHW052127110526
44592CB00013B/1776